Tracking Canids
Track and Trail Synopsis

Jim C. Halfpenny
Darren S. Ireland
Lara N. Bonn
Diann D. Thompson

**Tracker's Research Association
A Naturalist's World**

1998

Published January 23, 1998
Reprinted February 27, 2021

First Edition   2   3   4   5   6   7   8   9

ISBN: 9798714151200

Published in USA by

A Naturalist's World
PO Box 989
Gardiner, MT 59030
www.tracknature.com

Cover design by Amy F. Hahn

Suggested Citation:
Halfpenny, J.C., D.S. Ireland, L.N. Bonn, and D.D. Thompson. Tracking Canids: Track and Trail Synopsis. A Naturalist's World, Gardiner, MT 59030. 29 pages plus VIII.

CREATED IN MONTANA

Preface to reprinted edition of *Tracking Canids*

Sometime over 63 years ago, I read a book from my local library called *Animal Tracks and Hunter Signs* by Ernest Thompson Seton. Seton is arguably the "godfather" of tracking, as most trackers since his time can be traced to his inspiration. I, certainly, am one of those trackers Seton "Fathered." His book hooked me on natural history, especially tracking.

If you check the plaster casts in the Track Education Center Museum in Gardiner, you will find casts I made dated 1958. These are the oldest casts I still have; there may have been earlier ones though.

The casts are of raccoon tracks. Those raccoon casts carry a fond memory of Dabbles The Coon from *Animal Tracks and Hunter Signs*. Your assignment as a tracker is to read Dabbles' story and Seton's book. While you are at it, check out all the books by Seton!

Now I am in my 75th trip around the sun (74 on January 23, 2021) and my eighth decade of "following the trail." It is time to share the plethora of knowledge I have been fortunate enough to gain.

With the changing world, no one will ever get to live the life and walk the trails that I have. Few will ever track the seven continents, explore the tracking seasons and live nature at its prime as I have. Climate change helps guarantee my claim. I wish to share my experiences and hard-gained knowledge through a series of books called **Halfpenny Tracks**.

Halfpenny Tracks are publications about my lifetime of natural history and tracking experiences. *Tracking Canids* is but one of those books. *Tracking Canids* is for the hard core tracker who wishes to study in great detail tracks from the members of the wolf family: wolves, coyotes, fox and dogs. *Tracking Canids* is a student study project written in 1998 and represents an important contribution to tracking knowledge. Thus it is reprinted now. It is one of my database series of books which presents a large amount of detailed information.

The concept behind my database books is to provide enough data that the tracker can gain a detailed look at variation among tracks while following the trail. There will be other database books as time goes on. Now please enjoy this series and stay tuned for the next installment.

Special thanks are due to Darren Ireland and Lara Boon, Resident Students of A Naturalist's World, for their help in compiling the immense amount of data in this book. We compiled this book in 1998. Much, much more data has been collected since then but I am not sure if and when it will ever get compiled.

Most importantly I wish to thank Diann Thompson who has tracked many of the trails with me and has continually provided emotional support of my endeavors. Thank you my love!

ACKNOWLEDGEMENTS

This project has only been possible through the hard work and support of many people. It encompasses the field work of the Olaus and Adolph Murie and their families. The Murie collections are housed at the Murie Museum at Teton Science School. Richard Harris graciously granted access and use of the database that he and Robert Ream collected on domestics dogs. Diann Thompson, Jennifer and Brad Bennett tracked show dogs down our portable 16-foot sand box / runway at the dog shows making plaster casts as they went. Uncounted numbers of students have measured and trailed and sharpened my approach with their questions. Finally, Darren Ireland and Lara Bonn made possible this compilation with their tireless efforts at the computer, measuring, recording, graphing, analyzing and helping write summaries. There are others, who I may have forgotten to list specifically; blame it on age or a weak mind, but to them my sincere apologies. To all my heart felt thanks!

James C. Halfpenny

PREFACE

The preparation of this manuscript was made possible by two internships granted from the Tracker's Research Association (**TRAck**). TRAck is a research organization dedicated to providing

1) communication among trackers
2) continued opportunities for individuals to hone their tracking skills and knowledge
3) research into the science of tracking.

TRAck is conceived as a scientific organization designed to facilitate quality knowledge about the science of tracking. The scope of **TRAck** will span the broadest concept of the science conceived as including not only tracking skills, but the social, philosophical, and management aspects of tracking. All things, biological or not, making tracks may be investigated. Any topic relating to tracking from its origin and evolution to future refinements shall be included. Communications of **TRAck** will be through its newsletter, **TRAcks**.

To further tracking research, Jim Halfpenny and Diann Thompson, of A Naturalist's World, offer short-term tracking internships at their home in Gardiner, Montana, the north gate of Yellowstone.

TABLE OF CONTENTS

Please note, this book has been formatted to copy for use in classrooms. Therefore, page numbers were not placed on pages. Each page or section may be copied without page marring the copy. However, we ask that you leave our byline on the pages. Give credit where credit is due.

TRACKING CANIDS

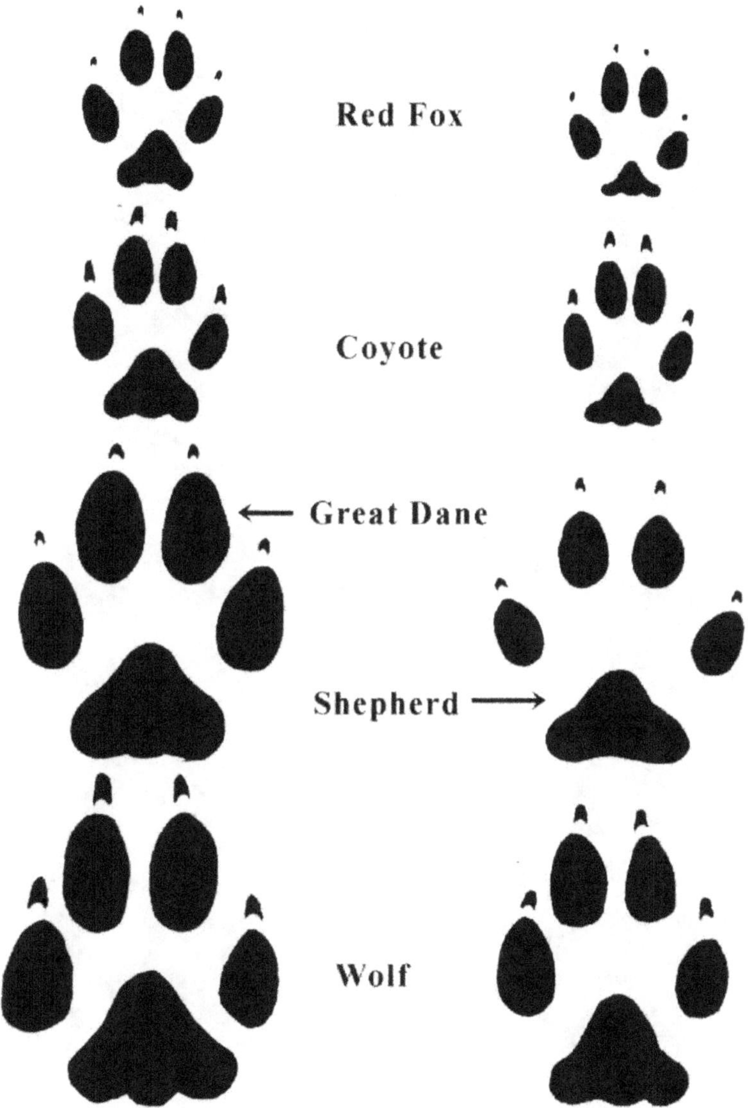

Tracks of four species of canids covered in this book: red fox, coyote, domestic dog, and wolf. Each track is drawn to scale for the average track of the species as determined within this book, then reduced in correct perspective to other tracks to fit on this page.

INTRODUCTION

Wolves of the world and their kin fascinate us, but most of the wild canids are seldom seen. Their presence is often only announced by a distant howl or a footprint along the trail. So keen is our desire for knowledge of the canids that every track sparks great interest. We want to know who has passed this way and what they were doing. Alas, identification is often difficult as the basic canid track pattern is relatively constant among species, differing mostly by size. Good footprint and trail measurements that encompass inherent variability caused by differences in size, sex, age, geographic region, and even breeds are lacking. Most books contain but a single listing of track sizes and gait patterns.

This book provides detailed tracking information on four canid species: red fox *Vulpes vulpes*), coyote (*Canis latrans*), wolf (*Canis lupus*), and domestic dogs (*Canis familiaris*). It is a compilation of, not only my 41 years of tracking (Halfpenny 1986, Halfpenny et al. 1995), but of tracking research done by Adolph Murie (1936), Olaus Murie (1952), Richard Harris, and Robert Ream (1983). From these sources, we provide the most detailed review of canid tracking ever undertaken.

The master database consists of 804 entries as follows: red fox - 48, coyote - 269, wolf - 308, and domestic dogs - 179. Eight hundred field entries represent countless, delightful field days, many at remote field sites strewn from Alaska to Hudson Bay, down the Rocky Mountains and through the deserts to the southern tip of Texas. Data contained here dates from 1940 to the present. Collections made by Olaus and Adolf Murie and their families are preserved today in the form of plaster casts which I measured.

To imagine, and then to design and conduct such a research project is beyond the current whims of research funding, graduate student time scales, and certainly would not meet the goals of most academic institutions. While basic natural history data are constantly in demand by wildlife biologists and ecologists, often they are not obtainable. This has been the situation with tracking data. Hopefully, Tracking Canids will provide a valuable contribution to the knowledge base of North American mammals.

But the job is not done! My emphasis through the years has been on wolves and coyotes. More data are needed for instance on the red fox. While I have yet to compile my data on kit, gray, and Arctic foxes, there too, more data are needed. Most of the dog information we have is from large dogs comparable in size to wolves or large coyotes. Information is needed on coyote- and fox-sized dogs. We need data that allows us to understand the differences in tracks created by different sexes, ages, and different regions. Who are the young researchers that will do this field research?

The format of the book, consists of separated Species Track Accounts for each canid and then comparison accounts for different combinations of species. Hidden within the master database is the information to answer many more questions that we have not had time to approach such as

1. discriminant analysis among species *1
2. growth curves for species
3. sexual differences
4. regional differences
5. and more

While I dream that someday I will have the time to answer these questions, I am willing to share the data with others who will make conduct proper studies and work on these and other questions.

James C. Halfpenny   ½¢

*1. Some references for using discriminant analysis in track analyses include Halfpenny et al. (1996), Halfpenny et al. (1995), Smallwood and Fitzhugh (1989), and Zielinski and Truex (1995).

METHODS

DATABASE:

 Field notes and laboratory measurements were compiled into a computer database listed by species. The master database is approximately 650,000 bytes in size. Supplementary databases were developed for each species or comparison analysis. Analyses and graphs were made on QuattroPro.

 Topics (data fields) listed in the master database are divided into five categories with data fields as follows:

Track Account (date, time, location, state, catalog number);

Animal (species, age, sex);

Method (measurement method, surface, quality, splay);

Footprints (foot, length, width, interdigital length, interdigital width, Toe 2 [length, width, inside claw length], Toe 3 [length, width, inside claw length], Toe 4 [length, width, inside claw length], Toe 5 [length, width, inside claw length], total length [includes outer claw length], gap length, inner toe width [both inner toes], outer claw width, inner claw width);

Gaits (gait code, gait, stride, group, intergroup, straddle, front straddle, hind straddle, overstep); and

Comments. For domestic dogs, the following additional data fields were listed: breed, breed code, weight. Values are not available for all fields due to impositions imparted on the tracker at the scene.

TERMS AND MEASUREMENTS:

 Terms used for track and trail measurements follow Halfpenny (1986), Halfpenny et al. (1995) and Muybridge (1899). For reference, measurements taken from footprints and trails are illustrated.

 To avoid problems with the depth to which a foot was pressed into the ground and to provide for standardization of track measurements, minimum outline measurements were used for most comparisons and analyses. Making minimum outline measurements is explained below in the article "How Big Is That Track," reprinted from **TRAcks**, 2(1):3, the journal of the Tracker's Research Association. The reprint may be copied for use with classes. For additional information, see Fjelline, D.P. and T.M. Mansfield (1989) and Halfpenny et al. (1995.)

Measurements of Footprints
Lengths and Widths

Toe measurements are made on Toe 3, which is second toe from inside

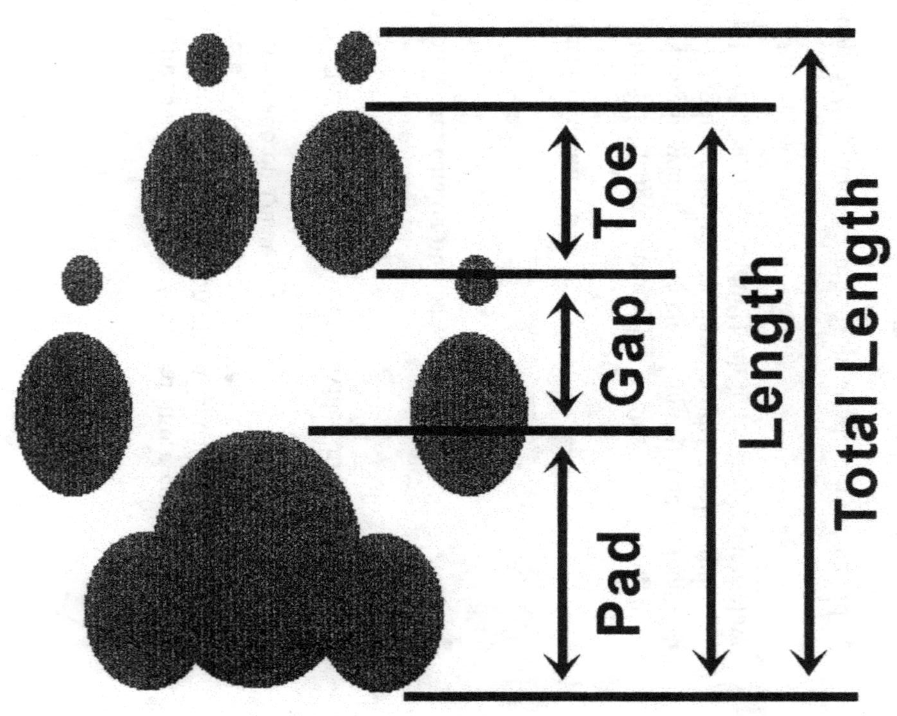

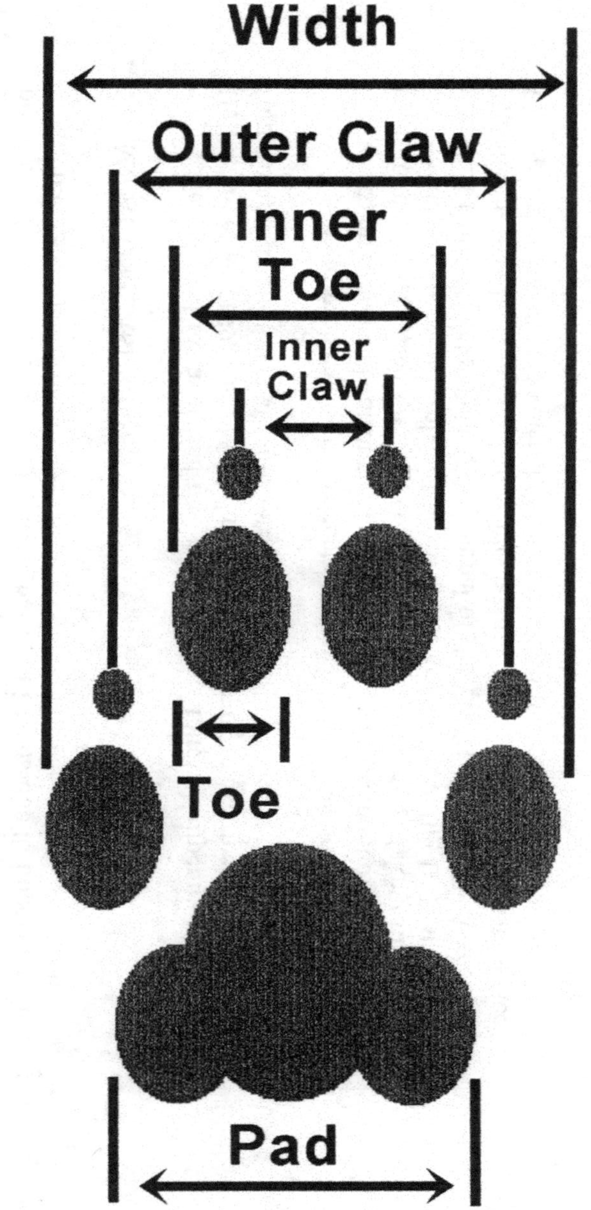

Trail Measurements

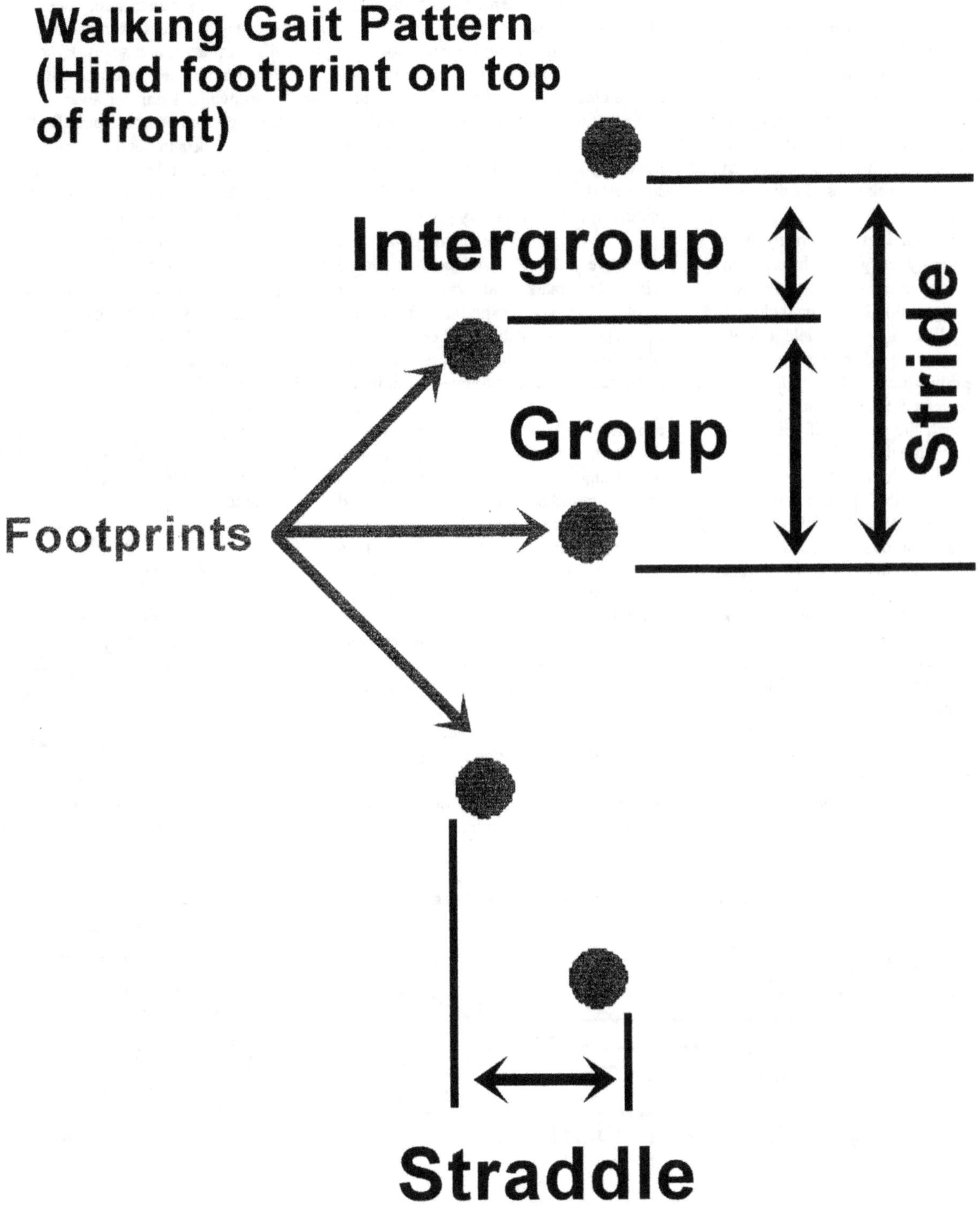

**Walking Gait Pattern
(Hind footprint on top
of front)**

Intergroup

Stride

Group

Footprints

Straddle

How Big is that Track?

Central to tracking is knowing how large a footprint is. This is a simple question until you think about it. One animal moving on a progressively softer surface will leave progressively larger tracks. What is the size of the animal's track?

Try this experiment. Place your hand on a hard surface, a table for instance. Feel the contact area of your hand with that surface. Imagine that contact area as your first contact with a mud surface. As your hand goes deeper into the mud, your hand print enlarges. Your hand can create an infinite number of track sizes, the deeper it goes into the mud.

Mountain lion and grizzly bear researchers jointly recognized the problem of variable track size and tried to develop means of over coming it. During their lion research, Fjelline and Mansfield (1989) developed a method for measuring tracks, we call the **minimum outline method.**

Remember the first contact area of your hand with the surface. If your hand went no deeper into that surface, your hand print would have only one size - the MINIMUM OUTLINE. If your hand sank deeper into the surface it would create a series of variable outlines as the mud flowed around the curved surface of your hand and fingers. All footprints have a minimum outline, but only prints that sink into a surface have variable outlines. Therefore, minimum outlines are the only constant and consistent size in tracking.

To measure the minimum outline, study the bottom of a print to determine where the rounded pad turns upward. The break point where the pad turns upward would be the minimum outline edge. Use this edge to measure tracks.

While the variable outline of a footprint may only be several millimeters wider than the minimum outline, those few millimeters have a large visual effect. The human eye sees area and area increases with the square of a linear measurement. In short, a few millimeters of width adds a lot of area to a footprint.

Minimum outline size does not change for different surfaces (assuming you have a clear track) and therefore provides cross-surface comparison, for example from snow to sand. While an animal may leave may sizes of footprints depending on surface, slope and speed, there is only one minimum outline for every print.

Assigning the break point is a subjective judgement and no two people will always mark it at exactly the same point. However, experimentation has shown that an individual tracker can reduce personal variation in measurements and that groups of trackers trained in minimum outline methods will become more consistent in their measurement of tracks. Quality measurements are the trackers goal and using minimum outline methods greatly reduces over-exaggeration and variability of track size.

Whenever someone tells you they have measured an especially large track, determine if they understand the effect of sinking into a surface. Be very cautious of any measurements where the measurer does not specify that an effort has been made to control for the foot sinking into the surface.

To report the track size for an **individual** animal, it is best to measure several different tracks and average them. A good report would also include a measure of variation (e.g. standard deviation). To do a good job of describing track size for a species, minimum outline measurements of several individuals should be averaged and variation measurements reported for both individuals and the species.

For your personal research and learning effort, develop a minimum outline set of measurements for species that you can easily access. Remember to measure different ages, and sexes. Even doing this for common pets, cats and dogs, would be worthwhile. I am not aware of any such data sets for household pets. Be the first on your block and send a copy to **TRAcks.** Also, once you have several measurements of different age animals, you can develop growth curves for footprint size.

A parting thought, be careful of any data set that lists only one measurement for a species. If it is an average, how many tracks and animals were averaged? What were their ages? What were their sexes? What was the variation in the data set? A range of measurements would be better, but the same questions still apply. Trackers must do quality work now days! You can help by developing good data sets and quality data sets take time to develop.

Area Exaggeration

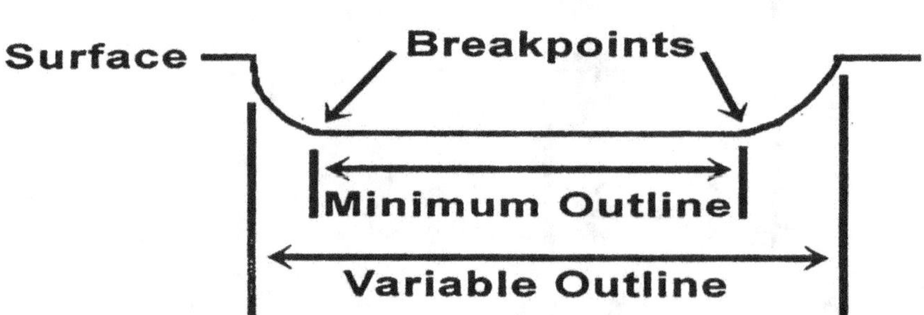

REFERENCE: Fjelline, D.P. and T.M. Mansfield. 1989. Method to standardize the procedure for measuring mountain lion tracks. In Smith, R.H. (Ed.). Proceeding of the third mountain lion workshop. 1988, Dec.6-8. Prescott ,AZ. Arizona Game and Fish Department.

REPRINTED FROM: TRAcks, 2(1):3, the journal of the **Tracker's Research Association**, www.tracknature.com, (406) 848-9458, PO Box 989, Gardiner, MT 59030. Article by Jim Halfpenny, Ph.D.

The database includes both minimum and variable outline measurements. Measurements made by Halfpenny prior to 1991 (including Halfpenny 1986) and those of Harris and Ream (1983) are variable outline measurements. To increase sample size, the variable outline measurements of Harris and Ream were used to characterize dogs and for comparisons of dogs with other species.

CUTOFF DIAGRAMS:

Cutoff diagrams were used to provide visual evidence of delineation between species. The species with the smaller footprint is always the line that starts at zero on the left of the graph and the species with the largest footprint is always the line that ends at zero on the left. Where the lines cross is the best measurement for separating species. This cutoff point represents the highest percentage of unknown tracks that would be correctly classified. To include a higher percentage of a species in the sample, simply move the cutoff point towards the species of concern.

RESULTS

Results are presented as Species Tracking Accounts containing independent graphs and explanatory text on the front and back of one sheet. These sheets may be copied for class or field use. However, we ask that you leave our byline on the pages. Give credit where credit is due.

Gray silhouette footprints were developed based on averages calculated for each species. The average length with claws (total length) and width were used to properly scale front and hind drawings. Drawings represent the average red fox and coyote from the intermountain west, the average wolf from North American and the average breeds as indicated. Gray track silhouettes may be copied for handouts.

Track Comparison Accounts were developed for breeds of dogs and between canid species. Footprints of domestic dogs were analyzed in greater detail than those of wild canids. One comparison sheet was developed for domestic dog comparisons.

Between species comparisons include fox versus coyote, coyote versus dog, and wolf versus dog. A comparison sheet was not developed for coyotes versus wolves because measurements of wolf footprints were so much larger than most coyote measurements. However, interdigital pad length and hind foot width overlap between coyotes and wolves. Overlap was small and a single cutoff criteria separates most tracks.

REFERENCES

Fjelline, D.P. and T. M. Mansfield. 1989. Method to standardize the procedure for measuring mountain lion tracks. Pages 49-51 in Smith, R.H. (ed). Proceedings of the Third Mountain Lion Workshop, Dec. 6-8, 1988, Prescott, AZ. Arizona Game and Fish Department.

Halfpenny, J.C., R.W Thompson, S.C. Morse, T. Holden, and P. Rezendes. 1996. Snow Tracking. Pages 91-163 in Zielinski, W., and T. Kucera. American Marten, Fisher, Lynx, and Wolverines: Survey Methods for Their Detection. U.S.D.A. Forest Service, Pacific Southwest Research Station, General Technical Report PSW-GTR-157. Phone 510-559-6300.

Halfpenny, J.C. 1995. Tracking Wolves: The Basics. Published Slide Show. A Naturalist's World. Gardiner, MT 59030.

Halfpenny, J.C. 1986. A Field Guide to Mammal Tracking in North America. Johnson Publishing Company, Boulder, CO.

Harris, R.B. and R.R. Ream. 1983. A method to aid in discrimination of tracks from wolves and dogs. L.N. Carbyn (ed.). Wolves in Canada and Alaska. Canadian Wildlife Service Report Series #45.

Muybridge, E. 1899. Animals in motion. Chapman and Hall, Ltd., London. Republished in 1957 by L.S. Brown, ed., Dover Publ., New York.

Murie, A. 1936. Following Fox Trails. University of Michigan, Museum of Zoology, Misc. Pub. 32.

Murie, O. 1954. A Field Guide to Animal Tracks. Peterson Field Guide Series, no. 9. Houghton Mifflin Company, Boston.

Rezendes, P. Tracking and the Art of Seeing: How to Read Animal Tracks and Sign. Camden House Publishing, Inc. Ferry Road, Charlotte VT 05445.

Smallwood, K.S., and E.L. Fitzhugh. 1989. Differentiating mountain lion and dog tracks. Pages 58-63 in Smith, R.H. (ed). Proceedings of the Third Mountain Lion Workshop, Dec. 6-8, 1988, Prescott, AZ. Arizona Game and Fish Department.

Zieleinski, W.J., and R. Turex. 1995. Distinguishing tracks of marten and fisher at track plate stations. Journal of Wildlife Management 59:571-579.

Red Fox *(Vulpes vulpes)*

Red Foxes are small-sized members of the wolf family (Canidae). The average red fox weighs 7.7-15.4 lbs while males weigh an average of 2.2 lbs more.

Red Foxes footprints, generally, are longer than wide; hind average 1.17 times longer and front footprints average 1.03 times longer. Front footprints average 49.9 by 48.5 mm (2.0 by 1.9 in). Hind footprints average 45.6 by 39.0 mm (1.8 by 1.5 in). Interdigital pads are wider than long; front footprints average 0.75 times wider and hind average 0.90 times wider. Front interdigital pad prints average 20.9 by 27.6 mm (0.8 by 1.1 in). Hind interdigital pad prints average 17.8 by 19.6 mm (0.7 by 0.8 in).

Red Foxes seldom walk. A rough idea of gait usage is obtained from recorded measurements. Walks represented 13% of the sample, trots 42%, and gallops 45%. Average strides for the main gait categories are walks - 54.6 cm (21.5 in.), trots - 84.1 cm (33.1 in.), and gallops - 159.2 cm (62.7 in.).   Note one lope (slow gallop) has a stride shorter than those of trots. Detailed stride breakdowns including the average, highest and lowest recorded values, 95% confidence limits are illustrated for 6 common gaits. The side trot is a common gait for red foxes averaging 92.4 cm (36.4 in.) compared to 80.5 cm (31.7 in.) for forward facing trots.

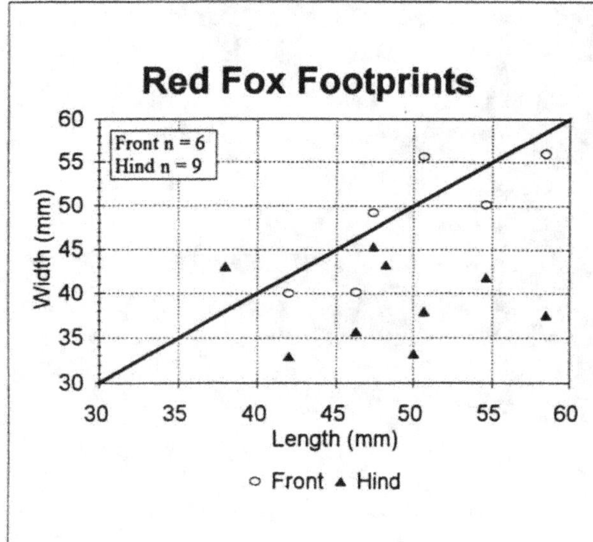

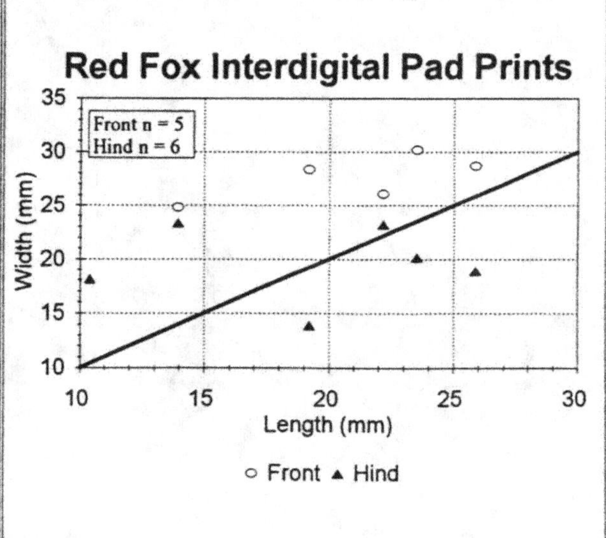

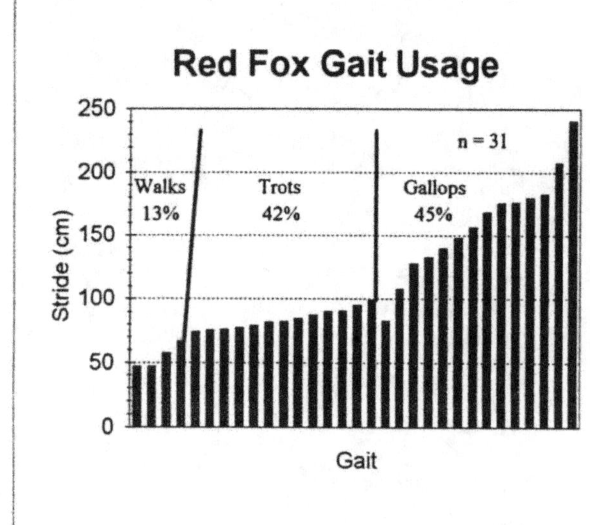

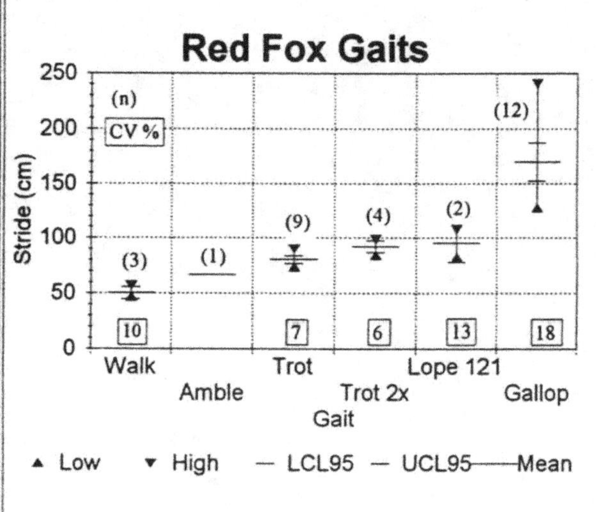

Characteristics of Red Fox Footprints and Trails

Statistic (mm)	Footprint Length with claw	Length	Width	Interdigital Length	Interdigital Width	Toe 3 Length	Toe 3 Width	Claw	Gap Length	Inner Toe Width	Inner Claw Width
Front Footprints											
Count	5	6	6	5	5	4	4	5	5	5	5
Mean	64.5	49.9	48.5	20.9	27.6	17.2	12.7	8.0	14.2	30.0	15.4
STD	8.18	5.45	6.49	4.10	1.91	2.82	1.82	2.62	5.72	2.94	2.71
CV	12.68	10.93	13.37	19.59	6.93	16.45	14.26	32.63	40.21	9.80	17.63
High	78.13	58.47	55.97	25.87	30.22	19.91	15.57	12.17	22.48	32.90	20.00
Low	53.16	42.00	40.00	13.96	24.85	12.49	10.50	4.23	6.21	24.64	11.91
Hind Footprints											
Count	5	9	9	6	6	6	6	5	6	6	6
Mean	52.9	45.6	39.0	17.8	19.6	15.7	11.9	4.9	13.9	24.6	10.0
STD	8.19	6.03	4.31	4.38	3.23	1.98	2.65	1.75	7.16	3.50	1.02
CV	15.48	13.23	11.04	24.62	16.48	12.60	22.33	35.41	51.32	14.24	10.17
High	65.43	53.70	45.40	24.03	23.35	18.41	14.93	7.82	29.40	29.50	11.79
Low	44.41	37.99	33.00	10.40	13.90	13.16	8.02	3.04	7.99	19.99	8.63

Gait	Statistic (cm)	Stride	Group	Intergroup	Straddle
Walk	Count	3			3
	Mean	50.5			11.5
	STD	4.95			1.79
	CV	9.80			15.52
	High	57.50			12.80
	Low	47.00			9.00
Amble	Count = 1	67.0			8.0
Trot	Count	9	8	8	8
	Mean	80.5	46.3	34.6	7.8
	STD	5.22	2.61	3.82	2.04
	CV	6.48	5.65	11.04	26.09
	High	90.30	49.40	40.90	11.10
	Low	74.20	42.30	27.50	4.60
Trot 2x	Count	4	4	4	4
	Mean	92.4	62.8	29.6	8.7
	STD	5.42	7.38	3.01	1.80
	CV	5.87	11.75	10.17	20.82
	High	99.06	74.30	33.00	11.35
	Low	84.50	53.80	24.77	6.30
Lope 121	Count	2	2	2	2
	Mean	95.5	70.3	25.2	11.1
	STD	12.55	10.75	1.80	1.65
	CV	13.15	15.30	7.14	14.93
	High	108.00	81.00	27.00	12.70
	Low	82.90	59.50	23.40	9.40
Gallop	Count	12	12	12	8
	Mean	169.8	105.6	64.2	12.0
	STD	31.09	15.80	22.55	1.93
	CV	18.30	14.96	35.12	16.03
	High	241.00	139.00	102.00	14.10
	Low	127.90	83.70	35.70	8.95

Coyote   *(Canis latrans)*

    Coyotes are medium-sized members of the wolf family (Canidae). In Yellowstone National Park, females average 27 lbs. and males average 33 lbs. Coyotes stand from 16 to 20 in. tall.

    Coyote footprints, generally, are longer than wide; hind footprints average 1.26 times longer and front footprints average 1.15 times longer. Front footprints average 64 by 56 mm (2.5 by 2.2 in.). Hind footprints average 58 by 47 mm (2.3 by 1.9 in.). Interdigital pads are wider than long; front footprints average 0.77 times wider and hind average 0.74 times wider. Front interdigital pad prints average 25 by 33 mm (1.0 by 1.3 in.). Hind interdigital pad prints average 19 by 27 mm (0.7 by 1.1 in.).

    Coyotes seldom walk. A rough idea of gait usage is obtained from recorded measurements. Walks represented 9% of the sample, trots 38%, and gallops 53%. Average strides for the main gait categories are walks -65.5 cm (25.8 in.), trots - 100.3 cm (39.5 in.), and gallops - 153.8 cm (60.6 in.). Note that some trots have strides shorter than those of walks, and some lopes (slow gallop) have strides shorter than those of trots. Detailed stride breakdowns including the average, highest and lowest recorded values, 95% confidence limits are illustrated for 8 common gaits. The side trot is a common gait for coyotes averaging 105.3 cm (41.5 in.) compared to 96.6 cm (38.0 in.) for forward facing trots.

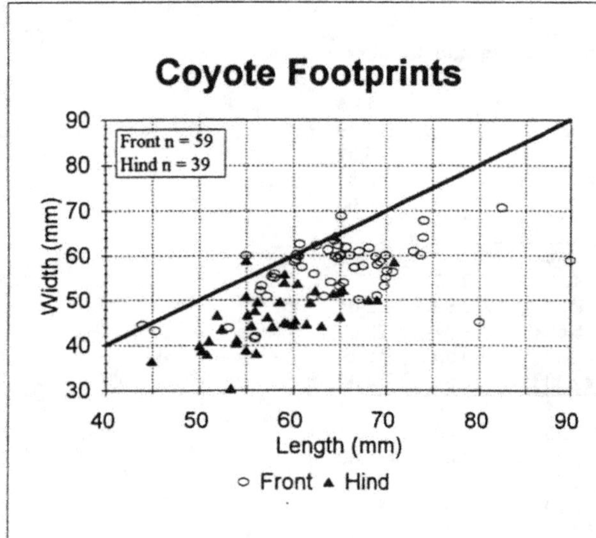

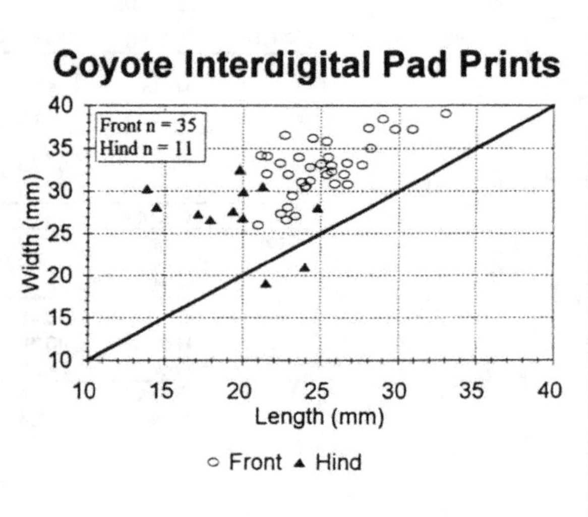

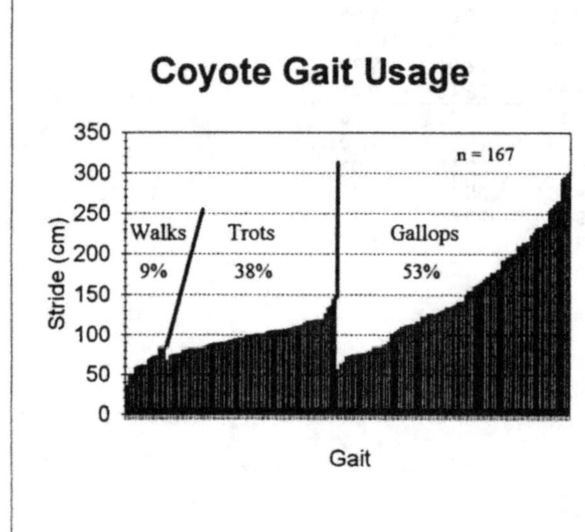

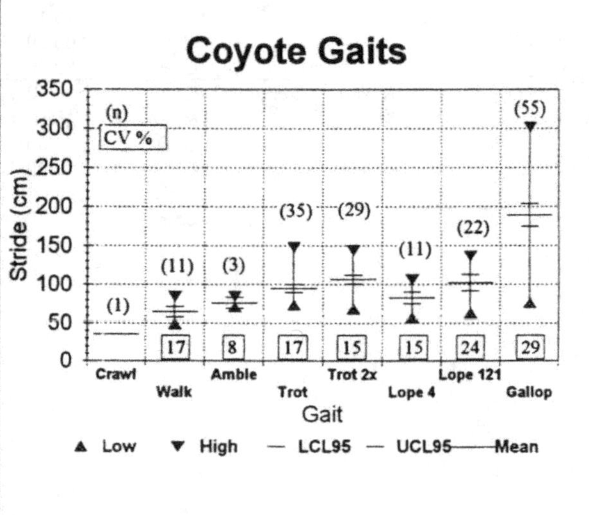

Characteristics of Coyote Footprints and Trails

Statistic (mm)	Footprint Length with claw	Footprint Length	Footprint Width	Interdigital Length	Interdigital Width	Toe 3 Length	Toe 3 Width	Claw	Gap Length	Inner Toe Width	Inner Claw Width
Front Footprints											
Count	25	58	57	35	36	28	27	10	26	26	23
Mean	76.4	64.6	56.5	25.1	32.8	20.7	14.5	5.8	18.2	32.6	18.4
STD	9.22	7.69	6.48	2.80	3.33	2.60	1.85	2.69	4.19	4.16	4.94
CV	12.06	11.91	11.46	11.16	10.16	12.56	12.76	46.14	22.98	12.76	26.84
High	91.00	90.00	70.75	33.06	39.04	25.48	18.81	9.94	24.60	40.75	26.30
Low	50.45	43.93	41.53	21.00	26.00	14.24	10.42	1.71	7.33	22.77	8.57
Hind Footprints											
Count	15	40	40	17	13	18	16	7	15	16	10
Mean	68.5	58.2	46.8	19.2	27.4	19.0	12.7	5.8	20.3	26.8	12.3
STD	5.81	5.65	6.68	2.82	3.55	3.82	2.61	2.26	3.91	4.33	3.03
CV	8.48	9.71	14.27	14.66	12.95	20.15	20.60	38.68	19.25	16.17	24.58
High	77.20	70.90	64.40	24.80	32.57	23.39	16.04	10.25	26.07	34.67	17.70
Low	52.48	44.93	30.48	13.85	19.11	6.00	4.00	3.35	10.98	16.20	7.95

Gait	Statistic (cm)	Stride	Group	Intergroup	Straddle
Crawl	Count=1	35.6			
Walk	Count	11	4	4	9
	Mean	65.2	46.0	27.3	12.6
	STD	11.39	6.45	6.51	3.33
	CV	17.47	14.03	23.86	26.34
	High	85.09	55.25	36.50	17.50
	Low	49.17	38.50	19.30	6.99
Amble	Count	3	3	3	2
	Mean	76.5	55.8	20.7	11.9
	STD	6.11	5.92	11.34	0.49
	CV	7.99	10.61	54.76	4.07
	High	85.00	62.99	36.50	12.40
	Low	71.00	48.50	10.41	11.43
Trot	Count	35	22	22	26
	Mean	94.9	59.0	36.4	9.9
	STD	16.28	13.73	7.41	2.14
	CV	17.16	23.28	20.37	21.60
	High	148.00	107.80	53.00	13.97
	Low	73.70	40.01	22.61	4.10
Trot 2x	Count	29	22	22	25
	Mean	106.8	64.7	42.1	14.2
	STD	15.86	21.23	16.14	13.74
	CV	14.85	32.82	38.37	96.68
	High	144.40	107.80	99.00	78.80
	Low	68.00	8.26	26.99	0.00
Lope 4	Count	11	10	9	9
	Mean	83.0	66.5	15.5	12.6
	STD	12.75	6.67	7.45	3.18
	CV	15.36	10.02	48.07	25.11
	High	106.70	74.70	34.00	17.00
	Low	57.00	50.00	7.00	4.80
Lope 121	Count	22	22	22	18
	Mean	102.4	76.8	25.6	12.3
	STD	24.60	11.60	16.23	3.40
	CV	24.02	15.10	63.40	27.60
	High	137.16	97.16	53.85	18.20
	Low	63.50	50.00	2.54	5.00
Gallop	Count	55	44	44	32
	Mean	189.2	121.7	74.3	12.3
	STD	55.01	38.09	30.02	5.67
	CV	29.08	31.30	40.41	45.95
	High	302.26	190.50	131.00	34.93
	Low	76.20	58.50	26.47	5.72

Wolf *(Canis lupus)*

Wolves are members of the family (Canidae). Female wolves introduced in Yellowstone National Park averaged 92 lbs. and males averaged 102 lbs. Wolves stand 30 in. tall on average.

Wolf footprints, generally, are longer than wide; hinds average 1.2 times longer and front footprints average 1.1 times longer. Front footprints average 106.0 by 96.5 mm (4.2 by 3.8 in.). Hind footprints average 96.1 by 83.7 mm (3.8 by 3.3 in.). Interdigital pads are wider than long; front footprints average 1.3 times wider and hind average 1.4 times wider. Front interdigital pad prints average 45.7 by 56.1 mm (1.8 by 2.2 in.). Hind interdigital pad prints average 37.8 by 51.3 mm (1.5 by 2.0 in.).

Wolves seldom walk. A rough idea of gait usage is obtained from recorded measurements. Walks represented 19% of the sample, trots 37%, and gallops 44%. Average strides for the main gait categories are walks - 129.2 cm (50.9 in.), trots - 149.2 cm (58.7 in.), and gallops - 257.7 cm (101.0 in.). Note that some trots have strides shorter than those of walks, and some lopes (slow gallop) have strides shorter than those of trots. Detailed stride breakdowns including the average, highest and lowest recorded values, 95% confidence limits are illustrated for 7 common gaits. The side trot is a common gait for wolves averaging 150.2 cm (59.1 in.) compared to 148.3 cm (58.4 in.) for forward facing trots.

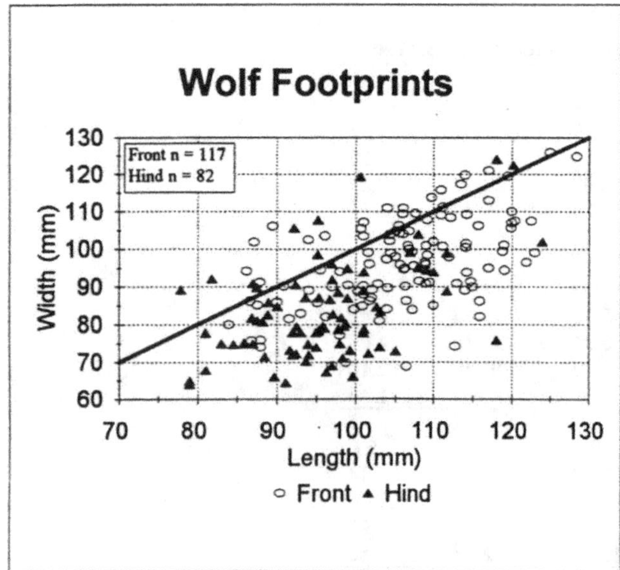

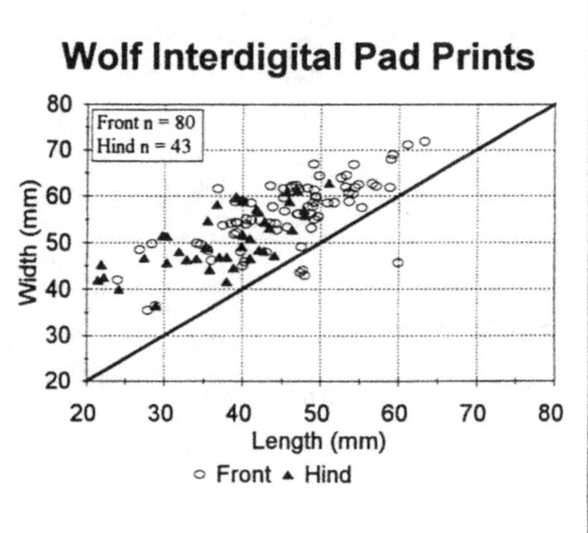

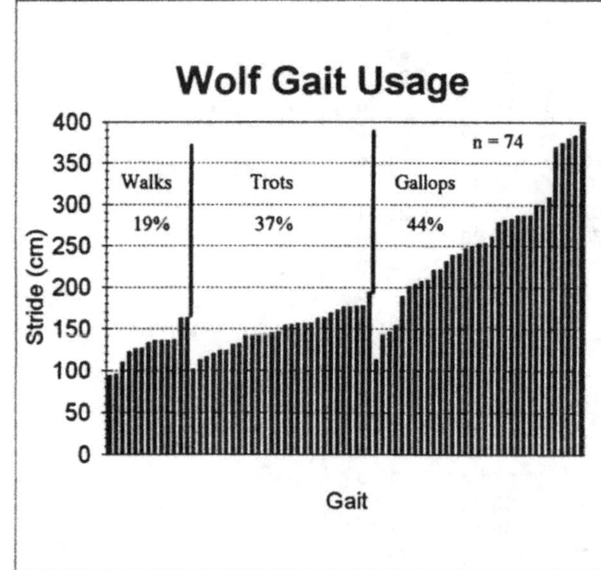

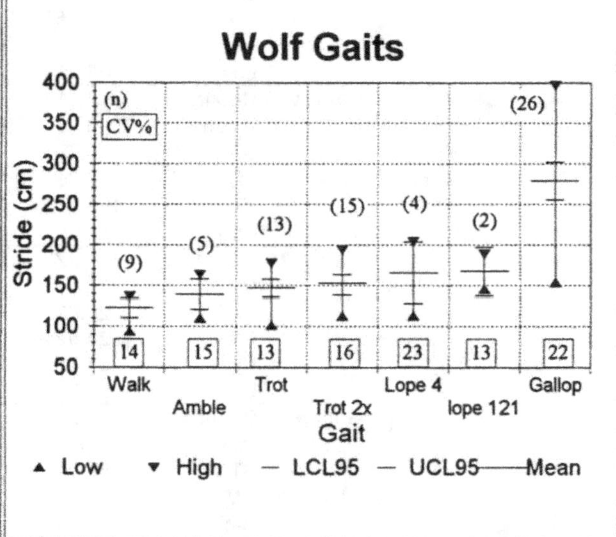

Characteristics of Wolf Footprints and Trails

Statistic (mm)	Footprint			Interdigital		Toe 3			Gap Length	Inner Toe Width	Inner Claw Width
	Length with claw	Length	Width	Length	Width	Length	Width	Claw			
Front Footprints											
Count	58	117	117	5	5	69	70	39	63	65	61
Mean	117.2	106.0	96.5	20.9	27.6	32.26	22.82	9.78	26.4	54.3	30.3
STD	10.58	9.63	11.90	4.10	1.91	3.07	2.67	3.32	6.70	4.80	8.77
CV	9.02	9.09	12.33	19.59	6.93	9.51	11.70	33.96	25.37	8.84	28.95
High	147.90	128.40	126.00	25.87	30.22	39.20	29.96	18.29	40.00	63.80	64.60
Low	94.00	84.00	68.80	13.96	24.85	24.17	17.25	3.57	11.95	42.60	13.50
Hind Footprints											
Count	34	82	82	6	6	40	44	24	37	38	32
Mean	109.1	96.1	83.7	17.8	19.6	30.1	21.2	8.5	27.2	49.9	24.4
STD	9.09	9.22	12.91	4.38	3.23	2.96	2.30	2.88	4.47	6.84	8.74
CV	8.33	9.60	15.43	24.62	16.48	9.85	10.83	33.76	16.43	13.71	35.79
High	134.62	124.00	124.00	24.03	23.35	36.01	27.09	15.20	39.02	60.62	46.50
Low	92.30	77.84	64.00	10.40	13.90	24.60	15.26	3.07	18.78	23.20	13.00

Gait	Statistic (cm)	Stride	Group	Intergroup	Straddle
Walk	Count	8	8	8	7
	Mean	122.9	73.5	49.4	17.8
	STD	17.09	10.11	8.27	2.74
	CV	13.90	13.75	16.74	15.42
	High	136.80	81.50	58.00	21.50
	Low	94.00	55.30	37.00	13.00
Amble	Count	5	5	5	4
	Mean	139.2	88.0	51.2	20.7
	STD	20.83	9.98	15.66	6.05
	CV	14.96	11.33	30.58	29.24
	High	163.50	104.50	69.85	28.91
	Low	110.10	77.00	23.20	13.00
Trot	Count	13	12	12	6
	Mean	147.2	90.0	57.4	17.0
	STD	19.45	17.25	8.35	3.52
	CV	13.21	19.18	14.56	20.70
	High	177.80	121.92	74.93	21.59
	Low	102.00	60.50	41.50	10.80
Trot 2x	Count	15	15	15	9
	Mean	150.9	99.2	51.8	20.7
	STD	24.62	19.50	10.17	4.93
	CV	16.31	19.66	19.65	23.82
	High	194.20	140.40	69.85	31.75
	Low	113.00	72.50	20.50	14.50
Lope 2	Count=1	254.0			
Lope 4	Count	4	4	4	
	Mean	165.5	119.2	46.3	
	STD	38.66	31.07	12.78	
	CV	23.36	26.06	27.64	
	High	204.40	153.40	55.70	
	Low	113.60	87.20	24.30	
Lope 121	Count	2	2	2	2
	Mean	167.7	116.7	50.9	23.7
	STD	21.35	27.30	5.95	1.20
	CV	12.73	23.39	11.67	5.05
	High	189.00	144.00	56.90	24.89
	Low	146.30	89.41	45.00	22.50
Gallop	Count	26	23	23	11.0
	Mean	279.0	193.7	91.6	16.9
	STD	60.49	45.90	31.03	8.2
	CV	21.68	23.70	33.86	48.5
	High	397.00	282.00	136.00	31.2
	Low	154.00	87.70	44.20	0.0

Dogs *(Canis familiaris)*

Dogs are variable-sized members of the wolf family (Canidae). The vary in size from the diminutive chihuahua to the giant mastiff and St. Bernards. Here, we consider medium to large sized dogs.

The average length of the front footprint slightly exceeds the width. Front footprints average 85.7 by 83.1 mm (3.4 by 3.3 in). Hind footprints average 78.0 by 67.9 mm (3.1 by 2.7 in). Interdigital pads are wider than long; front footprints average 1.3 times wider and hind average 1.4 times wider. Front interdigital pad prints average 37.3 by 49.6 mm (1.5 by 2.0 in). Hind interdigital pad prints average 29.6 by 39.9 mm (1.2 by 1.6 in).

Dog gait proportions are biased since mostly gallops were measured. Average strides for the main gait categories are walks - 66.3 cm (26.1 in.), trots - 136.3 cm (53.7 in.), and gallops - 184.1 cm (72.5 in.). Note that some lopes (slow gallop) have strides shorter than those of trots. Detailed stride breakdowns including the average, highest and lowest recorded values, 95% confidence limits are illustrated for 4 common gaits.

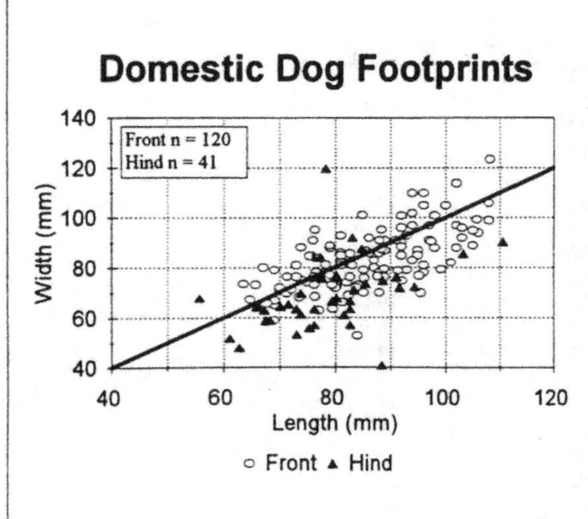

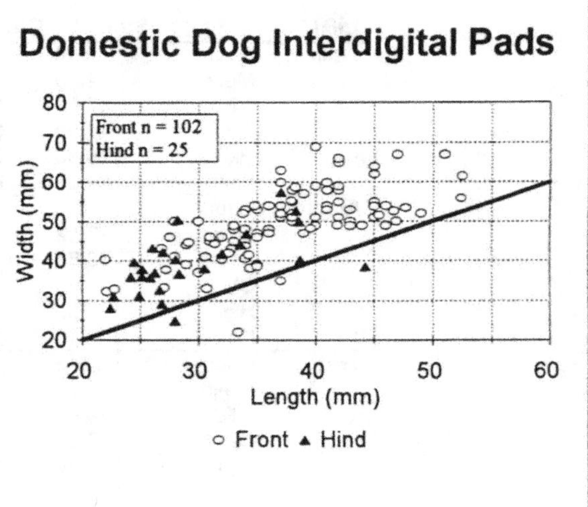

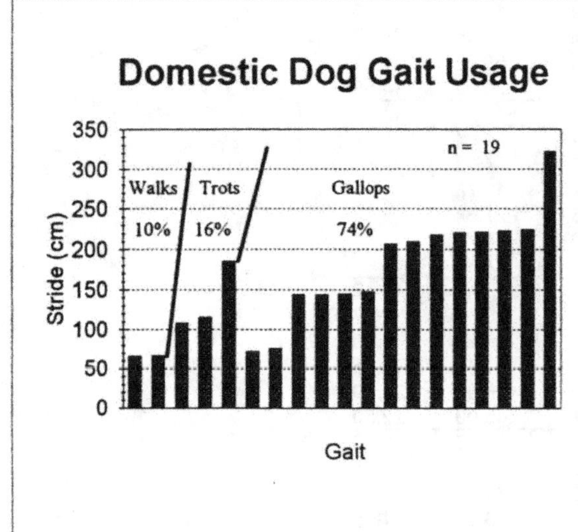

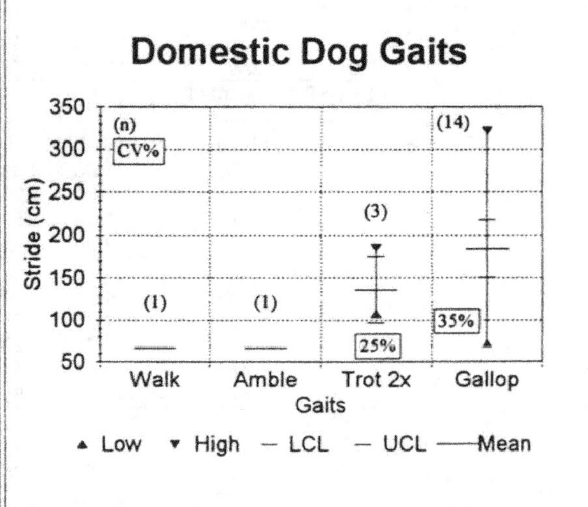

C:\1\TRACKDB\DOG.WB1 01/23/98 10:02:33 A Naturalist's World, (406) 848-9458, PO Box 989, Gardiner, MT 59030

Characteristics of Domestic Dog Footprints and Trails

Statistic (mm)	Footprint Length with claw	Length	Width	Interdigital Length	Interdigital Width	Toe 3 Length	Toe 3 Width	Claw	Gap Length	Inner Toe Width	Inner Claw Width
Front Footprints											
Count	109	121	120	103	107	108	108	36	102	109	99
Mean	101.0	85.7	83.1	37.3	49.6	31.0	20.8	6.3	31.9	48.4	24.9
STD	11.91	10.78	12.03	6.45	8.28	6.06	3.63	2.00	21.36	6.08	7.56
CV	11.79	12.58	14.48	17.30	16.70	19.56	17.46	31.76	66.93	12.57	30.44
High	134.90	108.20	123.40	52.50	69.00	44.00	31.00	11.10	118.70	65.00	72.80
Low	73.40	63.40	52.90	22.00	22.00	16.10	11.90	2.20	7.00	36.50	11.00
Hind Footprints											
Count	30	41	41	29	25	29	29	28	29	29	29
Mean	90.7	78.0	67.9	30.2	39.9	24.5	17.3	6.6	31.8	43.1	22.7
STD	12.00	10.67	10.30	6.60	7.22	5.58	2.91	2.83	38.73	5.95	4.98
CV	13.24	13.67	15.17	21.82	18.11	22.73	16.83	43.23	121.90	13.78	21.93
High	119.60	110.60	92.20	46.50	57.50	35.40	23.70	15.50	234.00	60.00	31.60
Low	68.00	55.70	48.20	20.10	28.10	14.00	12.30	0.60	9.40	35.50	16.00

Gait	Statistic (cm)	Stride	Group	Intergroup	Straddle
Walk	Count=1	66.0	29.0	37.0	11.0
Amble	Count=1	66.6	48.5	18.1	12.5
Trot 2x	Count	3	3	3	3
	Mean	136.3	98.4	37.6	11.9
	STD	34.62	33.55	3.61	1.84
	SE	19.99	19.37	2.08	1.06
	CV	25.41	34.08	9.60	15.54
	UCL	175.45	136.39	41.68	13.95
	LCL	97.09	60.47	33.52	9.78
	High	185.00	145.00	40.30	14.00
	Low	107.80	67.30	32.50	9.50
Gallop	Count	14	12	12	6
	Mean	184.1	120.3	65.7	16.4
	STD	64.24	50.14	26.41	2.32
	SE	17.17	14.48	7.62	0.95
	CV	34.88	41.68	40.21	14.18
	UCL	217.80	148.68	80.62	18.24
	LCL	150.50	91.93	50.73	14.52
	High	322.10	193.50	128.40	19.50
	Low	72.00	29.50	42.00	12.40

Gray Silhouette Tracks

Gray footprint silhouettes on the next two pages were developed based on averages calculated for each species. The average length with claws (total length) and width were used to properly scale front and hind drawings.

Front and Hind footprints
Red Fox
Coyote
Wolf

Front Footprints
Great Dane
German Shepherd

Red Fox Footprints (average size)

Front **Hind**

Coyote Footprints (average size)

Front **Hind**

Wolf Footprints

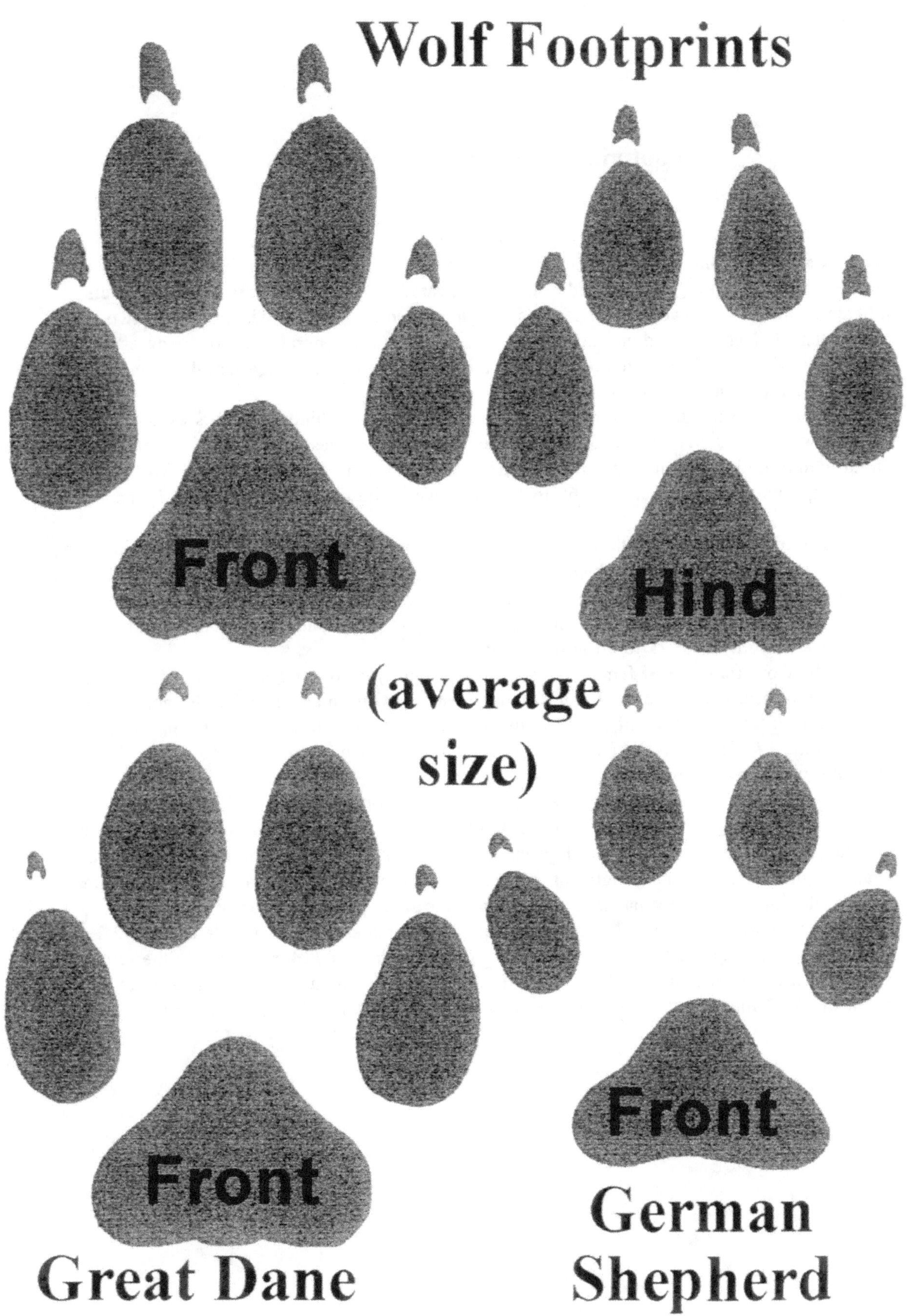

Footprints of Domestic Dog Breeds

Front footprints of domestic dogs were analyzed in detail because their larger size provides a better visual image that is easier to measure. Sixteen different breeds, two wolf/dog crosses and a group labeled mutt are indicated by different letters. Capitol letters indicate adults, while lower case letters indicate the juveniles (dogs under the age of two years). The 121 entries of domestic dog front feet follow the general trend of being as long as they are wide. A clearer picture of this relationship can be seen when length/width samples are represented by a single symbol.

Front footprints of the domestic dogs are larger than the hind footprints as is the case with the wild canids. The front footprint of domestic dogs ranges from 60 to 110 mm in length, while hind footprints typically span from 55 to 95 mm. In a comparison, widths of front footprints typically span from 60 to 120 mm, while the hind footprint width spans 40 to 95 mm.

The interdigital pad of the front footprint is larger than the interdigital pad of the hind footprint. Unlike the footprint which is longer than wide, the interdigital pad is wider than it is long. The front interdigital pad print ranges in length from 25 to 55 mm and typically spans a width of 30 to 70 mm. The hind interdigital pad print spans from about 25 to 40 mm in length and from about 25 to 60 mm in width.

The front footprint of female dogs span in length from 65 to 100 mm and for males, the front footprint ranges from 60 to 110 mm in length. Only males had feet longer than 100 mm. Front interdigital pads of females typically span a length from 25 to 45 mm and a width from 30 to 55 mm. The male front interdigital pad spans from 25 to 55 mm in length while the width spans from 30 to 70 mm.

Measurements of front footprints are summarized for different breeds. Where the sample size was large enough, breeds were divided by age and sex. In domestic dogs, males have larger footprints than females. For example, Alaskan malamutes, the female adult has a mean length with claw (total length) of 90.5 mm but the male adult has a mean length with claw of 98.6 mm. The German shepherd exhibits the same pattern; the adult male has an average length with claw of 101.7 mm while the adult female only has an average of 92.7 mm. The great dane adult male has a mean length with claw of 114.5 mm while the female only has a mean total length of 103.0 mm. For St. bernards, the adult male has a mean total length of 121.2 mm and the adult female has a mean length with claw of 114.5 mm.

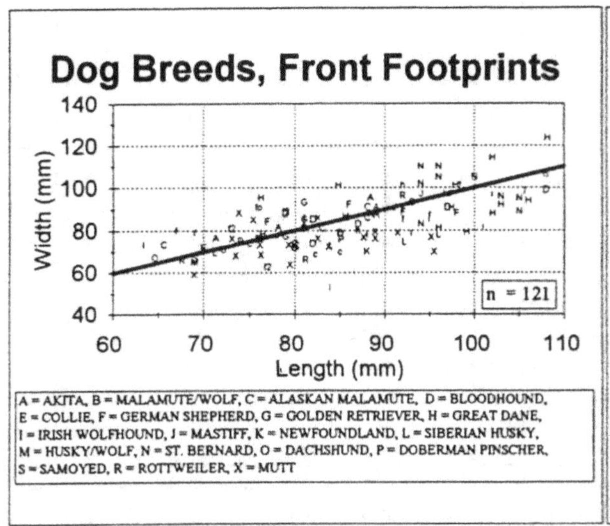

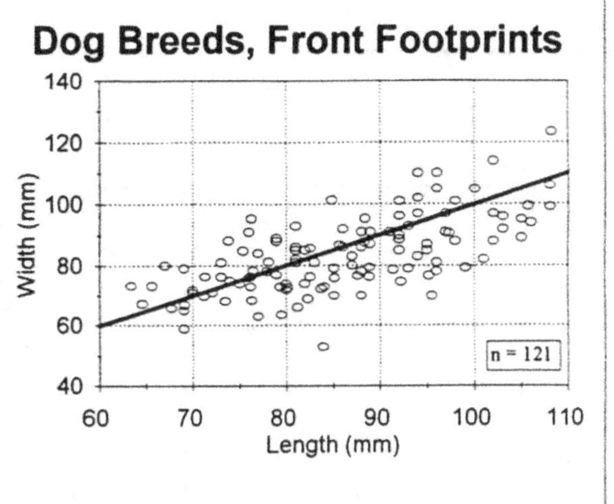

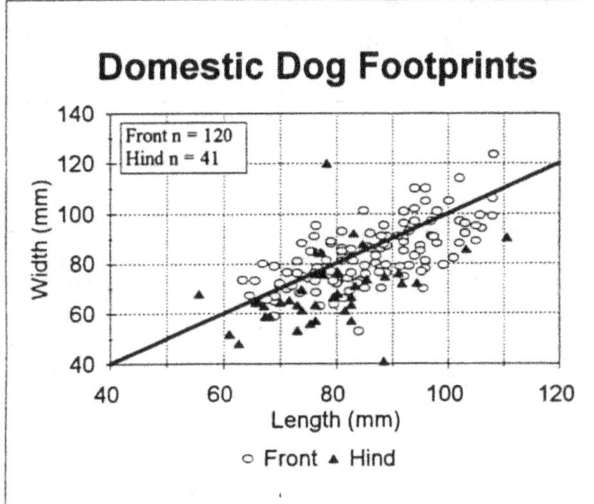

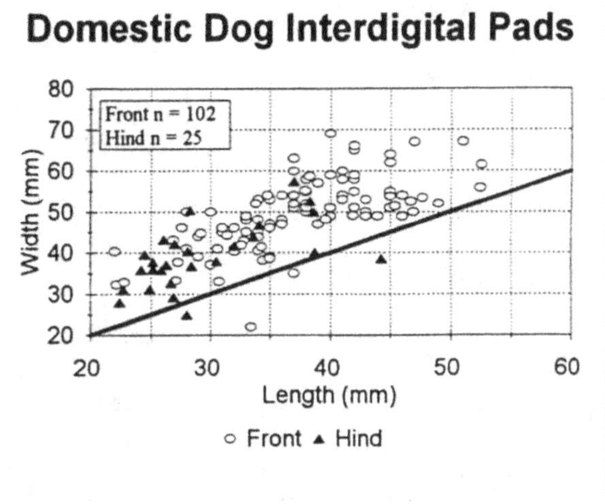

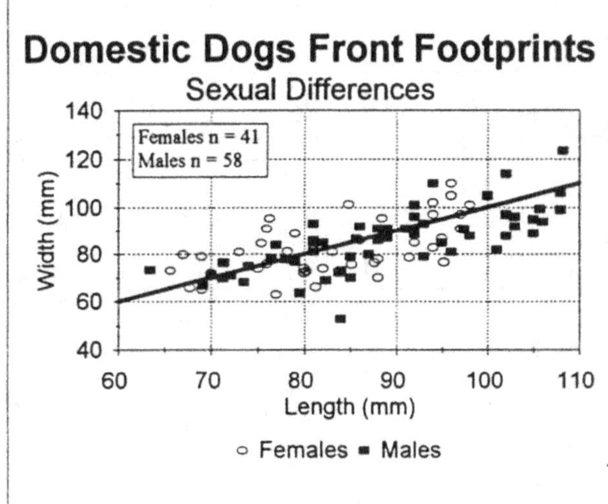

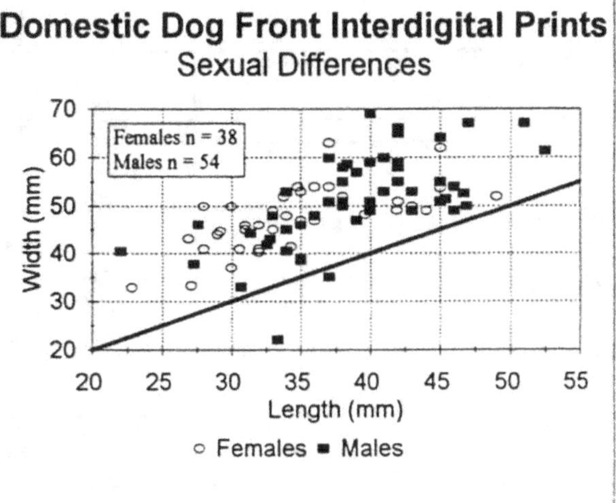

C:\1\TRACKDB\DOG.WB1 01/22/98 10:24:56 A Naturalist's World, (406) 848-9458, PO Box 989, Gardiner, MT 59030

Characteristics of Front Footprints of Different Breeds of Domestic Dogs

Breed	Statistics (mm)	Footprint Length with claw	Length	Width	Interdigital Length	Width	Gap Length	Inner Toe Width	Inner Claw Width	Weight (lbs)
AKITA	Count	5	5	5	5	5	5	5	4	5
	Mean	94.2	81.6	85.2	34.9	47.9	19.8	48.1	24.6	91.0
	STD	2.80	6.62	6.95	2.82	4.82	5.76	3.08	1.93	6.63
ALASKAN MALAMUTE/WOLF	Count	2	2	2	2	2	1	2	2	2
	Mean	92.0	77.5	78.0	34.0	43.5	20.0	47.0	30.5	58.5
	STD	2.00	3.50	3.00	1.00	4.50	0.00	1.00	0.50	1.50
ALASKAN MALAMUTE JUVENILE	Count	5	5	5	5	5	5	5	5	5
	Mean	92.0	78.1	74.2	33.5	47.2	17.7	45.0	28.0	60.4
	STD	6.60	5.30	3.89	3.74	1.59	7.30	3.38	5.22	19.71
ALASKAN MALAMUTE FEMALE ADULT	Count	4	4	4	4	4	4	4	4	3
	Mean	90.5	77.2	75.2	31.5	42.6	23.1	43.0	19.7	83.0
	STD	5.35	6.80	3.37	5.15	6.24	5.46	2.76	2.17	9.63
ALASKAN MALAMUTE MALE ADULT	Count	5	5	5	5	5	5	5	5	5
	Mean	98.6	87.2	85	41.8	52.8	22.4	49	25	82
	STD	5.35	3.66	8.07	3.31	1.60	17.53	3.41	5.97	10.30
BLOODHOUND	Count	9	9	9	9	9	9	9	8	6
	Mean	100.0	86.2	83.0	40.0	52.9	47.3	49.3	24.5	92.7
	STD	8.63	9.57	8.27	5.94	6.14	17.50	4.06	6.48	13.50
COLLIE		91.0	70.0	72.0	30.0	37.0	56.0	38.0	18.0	71.0
DACHSHUND			64.6	67.3						
DOBERMAN PINSCHER		98.5	85.1	75.8	30.6	41.0	19.0	42.6	16.6	72.0
GERMAN SHEPHERD JUVENILE	Count	4	4	4	3	4	3	4	4	4
	Mean	94.0	79.5	86.5	38.3	49.8	49.0	46.3	29.5	73.8
	STD	4.74	8.38	4.72	7.32	2.17	7.48	4.32	5.12	15.56
GERMAN SHEPHERD FEMALE ADULT	Count	6	6	6	6	6	6	6	5	6
	Mean	92.7	80.5	80.8	32.8	46.8	57.2	44.7	23.0	67.5
	STD	8.58	9.96	8.57	4.49	3.34	6.28	3.25	6.00	7.50
GERMAN SHEPHERD MALE ADULT	Count	4	4	4	3	4	4	4	3	4
	Mean	101.7	88.3	88.1	41.8	54.2	49.4	46.5	29.1	98.8
	STD	5.72	7.76	2.84	3.19	6.28	32.61	3.07	1.51	7.40
GOLDEN RETRIEVER MALE	Count	3	3	3	3	3	3	3	1	3
	Mean	94.0	80.3	85.0	38.0	48.3	53.3	48.0	32.0	70.0
	STD	5.72	0.94	6.53	2.94	3.40	7.54	1.41	0.00	8.16
GREAT DANE JUVENILE	Count	2	2	2	2	2	2	2	2	2
	Mean	111.5	100.0	103.5	41.5	59.5	23.5	53.0	31.0	142.5
	STD	3.50	8.00	2.50	3.50	4.50	12.50	1.00	1.00	17.50
GREAT DANE FEMALE ADULT	Count	4	4	4	3	4	3	4	4	4
	Mean	103.0	89.0	98.7	41.0	51.5	16.2	53.3	23.3	123.8
	STD	6.85	9.00	2.54	3.73	2.43	4.17	8.24	3.49	10.23
GREAT DANE MALE ADULT	Count	12	12	12	12	12	12	12	9	12
	Mean	114.5	96.0	91.2	41.6	48.8	20.1	55.3	25.7	157.4
	STD	9.15	9.13	13.40	4.76	11.56	10.36	4.01	3.15	20.52
MASTIFF	Count	3	3	3	3	3	3	3	3	3
	Mean	114.3	96.9	95.8	46.5	60.8	13.6	54.4	25.7	150.0
	STD	6.09	6.34	3.50	4.42	1.30	6.10	3.31	7.01	10.80
NEWFOUNDLAND		102.0	88.0	70.0		49.0		42.0		135.0
ROTTWEILER	Count	2	2	2	2	2	2	2	2	2
	Mean	96.4	79.9	81.0	36.3	42.4	69.7	46.6	47.1	95.0
	STD	4.70	12.15	15.20	9.15	9.15	49.00	5.10	25.70	7.00
SAMOYED	Count	4	4	4	4	4	4	4	4	2
	Mean	86.4	72.8	73.7	30.7	39.6	25.1	43.7	24.6	58.0
	STD	4.18	2.62	8.56	4.97	4.40	8.92	5.59	6.27	0.00
SIBERIAN HUSKY	Count	5	5	5	5	5	5	5	5	3
	Mean	92.3	81.4	73.8	39.0	48.4	16.6	43.7	23.9	53.3
	STD	11.55	12.37	2.65	10.81	5.92	5.70	2.23	2.92	17.00
SIBERIAN HUSKY/ WOLF		83.0	69.0	65.0	29.0	44.0	15.0	39.0	17.0	55.0
ST. BERNARD FEMALE ADULT	Count	4	4	4	3	3	3	4	4	4
	Mean	114.5	95.0	100.0	39.0	55.7	55.3	55.3	29.0	171.3
	STD	2.29	1.00	10.22	2.83	5.44	25.10	1.92	5.34	5.45
ST. BERNARD MALE ADULT	Count	5	5	5	4	5	4	5	5	5
	Mean	121.2	101.4	99.0	40.8	61.2	22.0	56.8	24.6	164.0
	STD	4.31	4.13	7.51	1.30	4.92	4.24	1.72	4.03	46.20
WOLFHOUND JUVENILE	Count	5	5	5	5	5	5	5	5	5
	Mean	113.2	95.4	85.8	38.0	57.0	40.2	50.0	17.6	134.0
	STD	6.79	5.82	6.11	3.41	6.48	23.66	5.02	5.08	18.55
WOLFHOUND ADULT	Count	3	3	3	3	2	3	3	3	3
	Mean	101.8	83.8	64.8	31.0	35.4	42.9	43.8	20.2	96.7
	STD	1.17	3.47	10.28	3.15	2.35	16.43	3.06	5.96	9.57
MUTT	Count	6	17	16	7	7	6	6	6	5
	Mean	99.3	83.2	75.4	33.8	47.7	24.6	44.8	20.0	94.0
	STD	6.98	7.47	6.55	3.76	5.93	4.44	4.11	5.46	14.97

Fox - Coyote Cutoff

Cutoff diagrams are used to identify the best point to differentiate between two species from a given measurement.   The best cutoff point for fox and coyote is where the two lines cross at 52mm.   At this point, approximately 80% of coyote hind footprints are longer, while 80% of fox hind footprints are shorter. The cutoff point can either be decreased or increased according to what percent of either species is to be included in the sample. If the cutoff were placed at 54mm in length, 100% of fox hind footprints would be shorter then this measurement, while 75% of coyote hind footprints would be longer. The cutoff point of 52mm yields the highest percent of correct identifications for each species.

The cutoff for fox and coyote hind footprint width is 42mm, with 71% of coyotes having wider hind feet and 71% of foxes having narrower. The best cutoff for interdigital pad length is 17mm, with 60% of each species on either side.   The best cutoff for interdigital pad width is 22mm, with 80% of each species on either side.

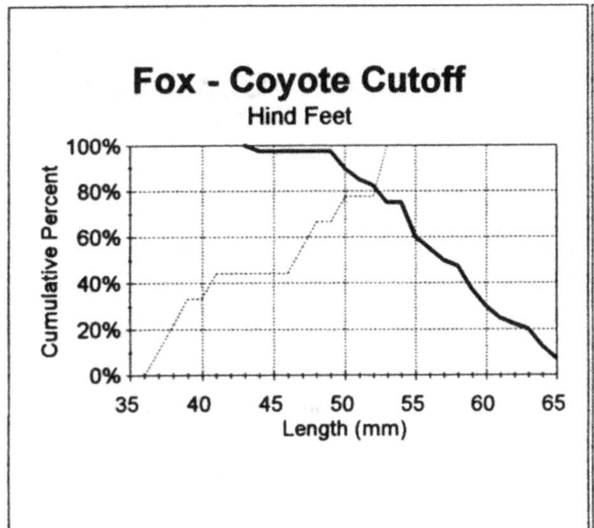

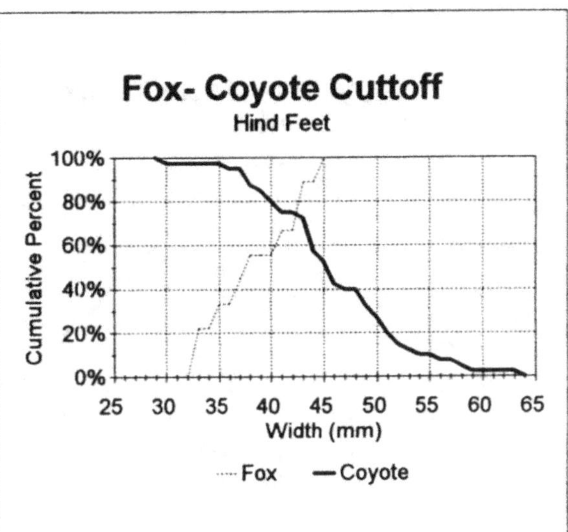

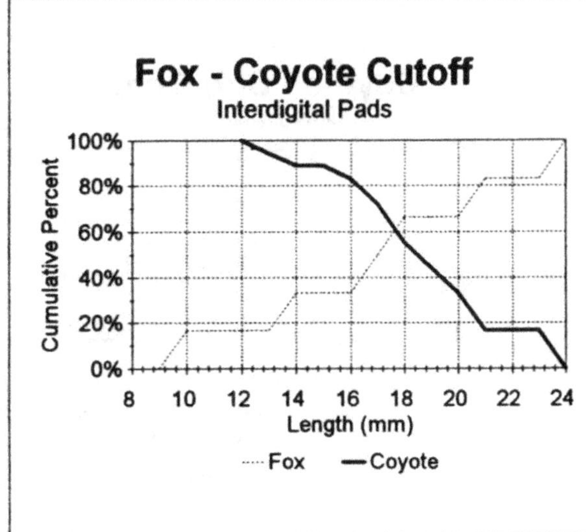

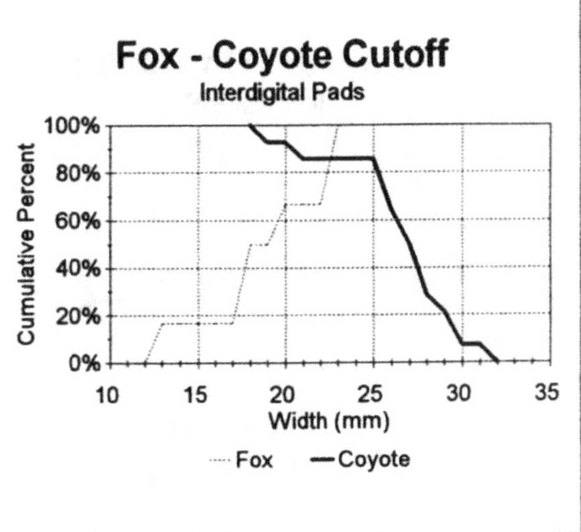

C:\1\TRACKDB\K9FOXCOY.WB1 01/04/80 15:07:48 A Naturalist's World, PO Box 989, Gardiner, MT 59715

Coyote - Domestic Dog Cutoff

Our databse only differentiates between large dogs and coyotes. The domestic dogs in this study were intended to be similar in size to a wolf, therefore they were generally larger than most coyotes. There are many breeds of dog which were not included in this study that will leave prints of a size much closer to prints left by a coyote. Additional data are needed for small dogs with foot lengths less than 70mm. These diagrams should only be applied for seperating large dogs from coyotes. For foot lengths less than 64mm, dog prints cannot be reliably differentiated from those made by coyotes.

Cutoff diagrams are used to identify the best point to differentiate between two species from a given measurement The best cutoff point for coyote and domestic dog is where the two lines cross at 64mm. At this point, 88% of domestic dog hind footprints are longer, while 88% of coyote hind footprints are shorter. The cutoff point can either be decreased or increased according to what percent of either species is to be included in the sample. If the cutoff were placed at 70mm in length, 100% of coyote hind footprints would be shorter than this measurement, while 88% of domestic dog hind footprints would be larger. The cutoff point of 64mm yields the highest percent of correct identifications for each species, 80%.

The cutoff for coyote and domestic dog hind footprint width is 54mm, with 90% of domestic dogs having wider hind feet and 90% of coyotes having narrower. The best cutoff for interdigital pad length is about 22mm, with 85% of each species on either side. The best cutoff for interdigital pad width is 31mm, with 84% of each species on either side.

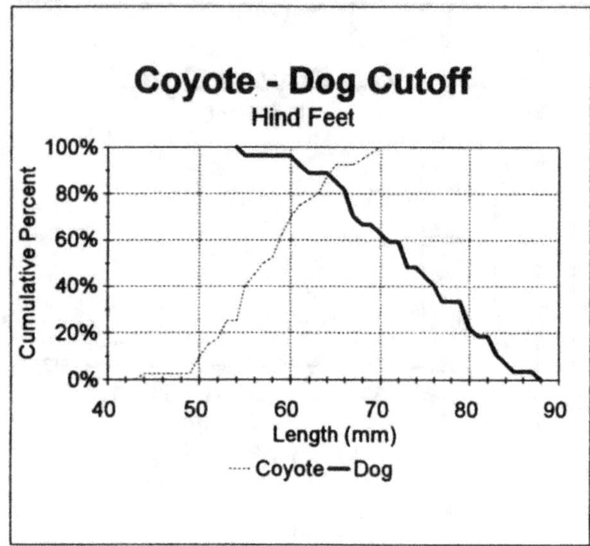

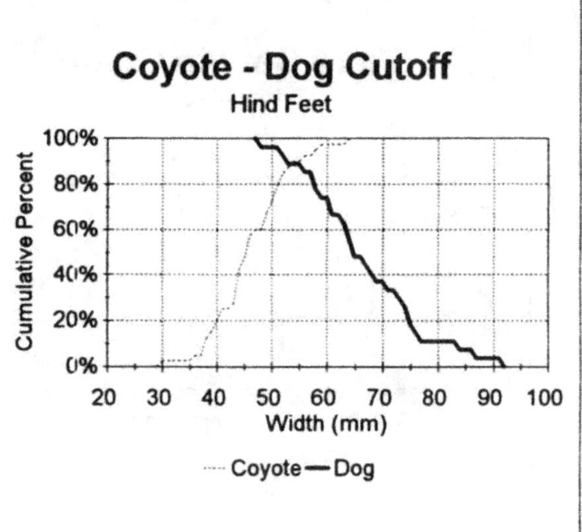

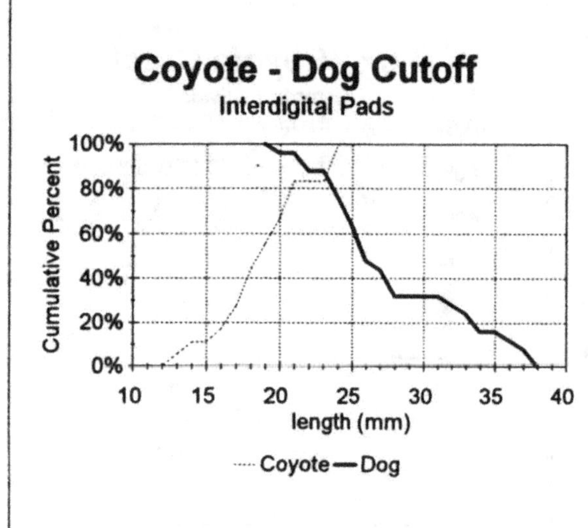

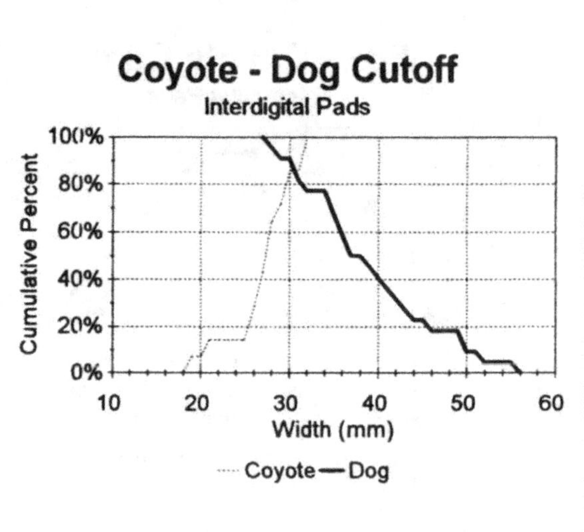

C:\1\TRACKDB\K9COYDOG.WB1 01/04/80 12:58:56 A Naturalist's World, PO Box 989, Gardiner, MT 59030

Domestic Dog - Wolf Cutoff

Cutoff diagrams are used to identify the best point to differentiate between two species from a given measurement The best cutoff point between domestic dog and wolf is where the two lines cross at 87mm. At this point, about 82% of wolf hind footprints are longer, while 82% of domestic dog hind footprints are shorter. The cutoff point can either be decreased or increased according to what percent of either species is to be included in the sample. If the cutoff were placed at 75mm in length, 100% of wolf hind footprints would be longer than this measurement, while 45% of domestic dog hind footprints would be shorter. The cutoff point of 87mm yields the highest percent of correct identification for each species, 82%.

The cutoff between wolf and domestic dog hind footprint width is 74mm, with 72% of wolves having wider hind feet and 72% of domestic dogs having narrower. The best cutoff for interdigital pad length is 33mm, with 70% of each species on either side. The best cutoff for interdigital pad width is 45mm, with 80% of each species on either side.

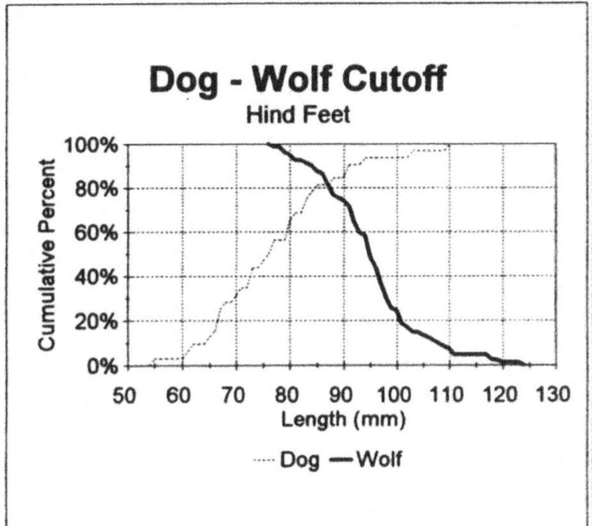

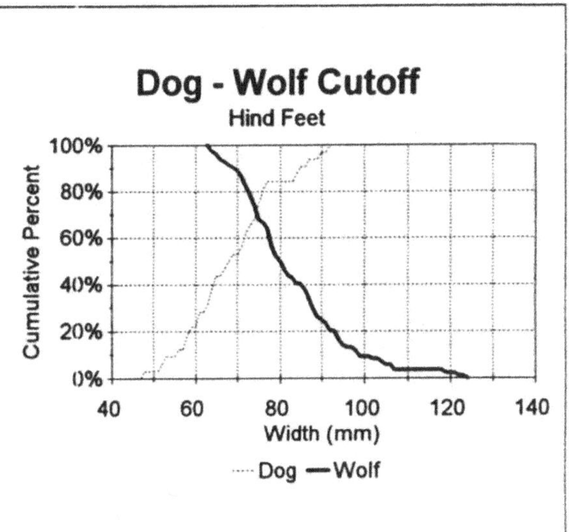

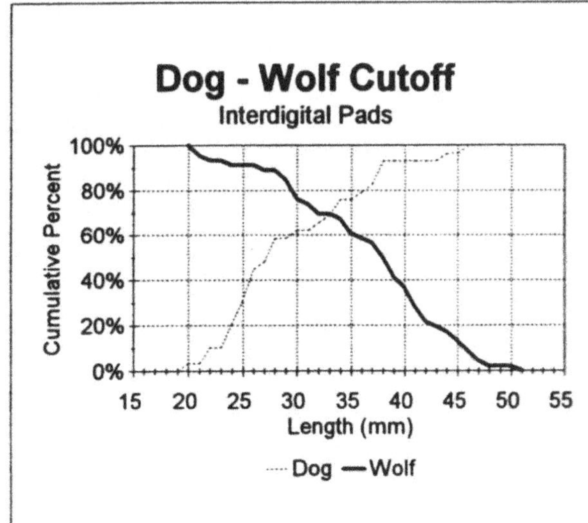

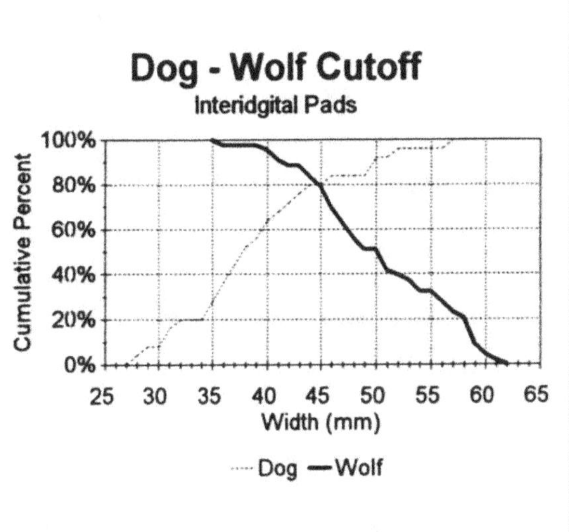

C:\1\TRACKDB\K9DOGWLF.WB1 01/04/80 13:15:24 A Naturalist's World, PO Box 989, Gardiner, MT 59715

Coyote - Wolf Cutoff

Coyote and wolf footprints differ substantially in size. Cutoffs for most measurements yield 100% of each species on either side.   For hind footprint length, the cutoff is 72mm. All coyote hind footprints are shorter than this, while all wolf hind footprints are longer. The cutoff for hind footprint width is 64mm, also with 100% of each species on either side.

Interdigital length is the only part of the footprint which showed any overlap of the two species. The best cutoff point of 22mm yields 12% of coyotes with longer interdigital pads and 5% of wolves with shorter interdigital pads. The best cutoff point for interdigital pad width is 24mm, with 100% of each species on either side.

